The Verdict

John Young

A LION BOOK

Oxford · Batavia · Sydney

Text copyright © 1990 John Young
This edition copyright © 1990 Lion Publishing
Cover illustration copyright © 1990 Jeffrey R Busch

Published by
Lion Publishing plc
Sandy Lane West, Littlemore, Oxford, England
ISBN 0 7459 1611 2
Lion Publishing Corporation
1705 Hubbard Avenue, Batavia, Illinois 60510, USA
ISBN 0 7459 1611 2
Albatross Books Pty Ltd
PO Box 320, Sutherland, NSW 2232, Australia
ISBN 0 7324 0212 3

First edition 1990

Acknowledgments
Benedettine di Priscilla, pages 32-33; Birmingham Post and Mail, page
27; Jeffrey R Busch, page 41; Mary Evans Picture Library, page 9;
Lion Publishing/David Alexander, pages 5 , 20-21;
Topham Picture Library, page 39; Vatican Museum, page 13; Zefa
(UK) Ltd, pages 24-25, 44-45

Printed and bound in Yugoslavia

Contents

1

A Real Person?

We acknowledge Jesus every time we write the date — any date. For we organize our entire history with reference to his birth. But are the ancient Bible stories about him true? Why did he die? Can we really accept that he rose from the dead? And what does it all mean for us today? These are some of the questions examined in this book.

Because of his tremendous influence, his life has been studied more closely than others. So it is not surprising that a few writers have tried to grab sensational headlines with controversial claims. One claim which surfaces from time to time is that Jesus did not really exist. Clearly, this claim strikes at the foundations of Christian belief.

It is true that most of the ancient written evidence about Jesus came from Christian quills. It is also true that the Roman authorities, who were very sensitive to popular uprisings, were more interested in the *followers* of Jesus than in Jesus

The Garden Tomb in Jerusalem. After his crucifixion, Jesus was buried in such a tomb. But his followers, then and now, claim he rose from the dead.

himself. So what hard evidence do we have for Jesus' life?

The Jewish historian Josephus twice referred to Jesus — noting his teaching, reported miracles and death on the cross. And, early in the second century, we find Roman officials and historians (Tacitus, Suetonius and Pliny) writing about the Christian movement. They noted this troublesome new sect, which they believed to originate with someone known as 'Christ'.

In addition to what Josephus and the Roman authorities said, we must look at what the Jewish leaders did *not* say. Jesus and his first disciples were Jews. But many of their own people opposed them, especially when the new movement grew rapidly after Jesus' death. So we find ancient Jewish writers saying harsh things against Jesus.

If these writers could have shown that Jesus was invented, they would have won their argument hands down. But they knew that he *had* lived and what he taught. Indeed, they acknowledged that he performed miracles. So, much as they disliked all that Jesus stood for, they did not waste time arguing about his existence. They knew that Jesus was fact not fiction.

Today we find people who disagree with the views of the Christian church but cannot dismiss the fact of Jesus' life. Many non-Christian writers have been fascinated and deeply impressed by him.

□ The Marxist Milan Machovec, in his book about Jesus, acknowledges that Jesus 'set the world on fire', and he explains why. 'He himself was the attraction. They saw in him a man who already belonged to this coming kingdom of God; they saw what it meant to be full of grace.'

□ The Jewish scholar Geza Vermes speaks warmly of Jesus. He describes him as 'an unsurpassed master of the art of laying bare the inmost core of spiritual truth'.

The Conspiracy Theory

Those who say that Jesus is fiction not fact require us to believe in a conspiracy, that:

- the first Christians were very creative inventors,
- their message about truth was based upon a lie,
- not a single member of the conspiracy broke ranks and told the truth,
- these inventors were foolish enough to suffer and die for their fabricated stories,
- their skills were so great that they were able to hoodwink people in every generation,
- the whole western world has been so taken in by their hoax that it has based its calendar upon this fiction.

It seems much more likely that they were impressed and challenged by a real person.

To invent Jesus would require someone of the stature of Jesus.

A Marxist and a Jew. Neither is biased towards Christianity. Both are honest witnesses with no Christian axe to grind. Yet they admit that Jesus has made a tremendous impression upon them. They find him fascinating, solid and real. Fact, not fiction.

2

A Virgin Birth?

We would expect the most famous story ever told to be remarkable. We are not mistaken. The cast is impressive: animals and shepherds, camels and kings, a mysterious star and a heavenly choir.

The plot is action-packed. Murder and attempted murder. A thwarted, wicked king. A narrow escape — and a dangerous journey into exile.

Central to this story are a pregnant woman, an anxious man and a difficult journey. 'No Vacancies'. 'House Full'. Eventually they find a shelter and the baby is born. They lay him in a borrowed manger.

The anxious couple have become as famous as their son. Joseph and Mary. The Virgin Mary. Now the Bible nowhere speaks about a virgin birth. Jesus' birth was normal. It was his conception which has caused all the fuss. The Gospel writers claim that no human father was involved. It was

Wise men and shepherds, a guiding star and a stable. Are the accounts of Jesus' birth more than fairy tales?

God himself who caused the baby to grow in Mary, for the usual nine months. In other words, it was a miracle.

Naturally enough, some people find this hard to believe. Alternative explanations are not too hard to find. Mary and Joseph would not be the first engaged couple to conceive a child. Or perhaps a man other than Joseph had found Mary attractive . . . Indeed, this was Joseph's initial reaction on hearing that Mary was pregnant.

If it was as straightforward as that, the usual options would apply. Joseph would break off the engagement. Or he would bring forward the date of the wedding. Or they would face a hostile world together.

Instead we find a delicate and lovely story. A story about angels and dreams. A story which fulfills a prophecy. A story about a virgin who conceives a baby.

As a cover-up, it is laughable. Throughout the centuries many engaged couples have been dismayed to find a baby on its way. But no couple has cooked up a story like this, and been believed.

But this story *is* widely believed. Why? — because of the unique baby. Or rather, because of the unique man who grew from the baby.

In some ways Jesus was very normal. He worked and slept, ate and drank, and experienced a wide range of emotions.

But he was soon recognized as unique. The early Christians came to acknowledge him as teacher and prophet — and as Lord and God, the light and hope of the world. They came to see that it was logical for a unique man to have a unique conception.

Pagan stories about virgins giving birth to gods circulated in the ancient world. And some now suggest that the stories about Jesus' remarkable birth grew up as a *result* of his later importance. But Jesus was born into a Jewish family, in a Jewish society. And the Jews strongly disliked pagan stories about gods. They regarded them as blasphemous fables.

It is very unlikely indeed that a Jewish writer such as Matthew would invent such a story. It would create more problems than it would solve.

Besides, nothing in the Bible is built upon the virgin birth. It is stated without any 'therefores'. Perhaps it is recorded simply because it happened.

3

An Accurate Account?

In the four Gospels, Jesus makes wonderful promises. He speaks of the love and grace of God. He offers eternal life and forgiveness for our sins.

But he also makes very tough demands about the way we live, the way we use our time, energy and money, and the way we conduct our relationships.

He offers to us a new life. He demands from us a new lifestyle.

The stakes are high. So it is only sensible for us to ask for evidence. Do the Gospels give us an accurate record of Jesus' life, miracles and teaching?

We cannot be sure precisely when the Gospels were written. We *can* be sure that they were written within the lifetimes of some of Jesus'

The Gospels survived through being repeatedly copied. There are thousands of ancient manuscripts in existence, reaching back almost to the first century.

ΕΡΙΤΟΥΤΩΝ ΕΝΑΙΟ ΕϹΤΙΝ
ΟΠΟΙΗΤΑΠ̅Ι̅Ρ̅Α̅ ΛΟΓΙΛΛΛΦΕΙϹ
ΛΛΟΤΗΡΙΚΤΟΙ ϹΤΡΕΒΛΩϹΟΥ
ΙΟΚΑΙΛϹΤΥΠΛΕΡΕΛΦΛϹΠΡΟϹΤΗ
ΖΙΛΝ ΕΛΥΤΩΝΛΠΩΛΕΙΛΝ
ΜΕΙϹΟΥΝΛϹΛΛΠΙΤΗΤΟΙΠΡΟ
ΟΝΤΕϹ ΦΥΛΛϹϹΕϹΘ Ι̅ΝΛΜΗΤ
ΩΝΛΘΕϹΜΩΝ ΠΛΛΝΗϹΥΝ
ΘΕΝΤΕϹ ΕΚΠΙΠΕϹΗΤΕΤΟΥΙΔΙΟ
ΤΗΡΙΓΜΟΥ ΛΥΖΛΝΕϹΘΕΛΕΕΝΧΛ
ΗΓΝΩϹΗΤΟΥ Κ̅Υ̅ ΗΜΩΝ ΚΛ
ΩΤΗΡΟϹ Ι̅Η̅Υ̅ Χ̅Υ̅ ΛΥΤΩΗΔΟ
ΝΝΥΝ ΚΛΙϹΗΜΕΡ ΛΙ̅ΩΝΟϹ

┌─────────────────────────────┐
│ ΠΕΤΡΟΥ ΕΠΙϹΤΟΛΗ Β̅ │
└─────────────────────────────┘

ΕΙΡΗΝΗΤΩΓΡΛΦΛΝΤΙ
Κ̅ΛΥΤΩΛΝΛΓΙΝΩϹΚΟΝΤΙ

disciples. We *can* be sure that the stories about Jesus were told and retold before they were written down. We *can* be sure that Eastern memories were very well trained. In the centuries before widespread book reading, information was learnt by heart.

It would have been difficult to invent material about Jesus without risking contradiction by people who had actually seen and heard him.

There are other factors, too, which suggest the Gospels are accurate:

□ **The question of truth.** One strong element in the reported teaching of Jesus is the importance of truthfulness. It is hard to imagine that this highly moral teaching would be based on a lie or gross distortion.

□ **The fact of suffering.** Many of Jesus' early disciples suffered for their faith. Some even died. People will not willingly — even joyfully — suffer for something they helped to invent.

□ **The reputation of the apostles.** If the Gospels were an invention, the early church leaders would have been involved in the conspiracy. Yet the Gospels do not show them in a good light. They were slow to understand, and they let Jesus down badly. This is strange material for ambitious inventors!

□ **The cleverness factor.** It would have taken someone as great as Jesus to invent the teaching of Jesus. So why bother with a complicated cover-up?

Why not deliver the teaching yourself, and gather your own followers? Again, a conspiracy theory does not fit the facts.

☐ **Archaeology.** Archaeologists have not dug up anything like a plaque which says 'Jesus of Nazareth lived here', but they do support a general confidence in the Gospel records.

We do not have the actual papyrus on which Mark wrote his Gospel — nor the paper on which Shakespeare wrote his plays. To decide whether we have accurate copies of ancient documents, experts ask two questions:

1. How many copies do we have?
2. How near in time are the copies to the original document?

When compared with all other important ancient writings, the New Testament is in a league on its own. For other ancient documents, such as Caesar's *Gallic War* or Tacitus' *Histories*, we have a dozen ancient copies at most. These are dated 700 years or more after the original. With the Gospels we have literally thousands of ancient copies. And the time gap is much closer — only 150 years in one case, with one fragment going back even to AD130.

The Gospel Story

Jesus was born in Bethlehem, about five miles south of Jerusalem, and a long way from his family home. Mary and Joseph journeyed there for a compulsory census organized by the powerful Romans, during the reign of the Emperor Augustus Caesar.

King Herod heard about this new infant 'king' from a group of Eastern wise men who were guided by a mysterious star. They had come to revere the child, but Herod feared a dangerous rival and tried to kill Jesus.

The family escaped to Egypt and, when Herod died, they returned to Nazareth in Galilee — a northern region of Palestine. There Joseph worked as a carpenter. We know little more about Jesus until he started preaching around the age of thirty. For three years he journeyed with a group of twelve disciples. He had many other supporters, including several women.

Jesus became famous for his remarkable teaching, several reported miracles, and sharp conflict with the authorities. They felt threatened by his popularity and, eventually, succeeded in having him arrested and tried.

Pontius Pilate, the Roman governor, held Jesus to be innocent of the charges made by the religious leaders. He wanted to release Jesus. But under pressure from the crowds, he ordered death by crucifixion. He distanced himself from this decision by washing his hands in public.

Jesus was laid to rest in the tomb of Joseph of Arimathea, one of his few influential followers. Three days later, the Bible claims, he rose from the dead.

Jesus was born in obscurity and executed as a criminal. The chances of him becoming the most famous person in all history were very small. But what had seemed like the end, was really the beginning.

4

Unique Teaching?

The four Gospels contain Jesus' teaching. As he moved from his home in rural Galilee to the nation's power-base in sophisticated Jerusalem, he adapted his style to his audience.

Jesus' hearers were struck by the content of his teaching, which concentrated on the Kingdom of God. He was conscious of standing in a God-given stream of teaching. He used stories and parables like other teachers, but he challenged many entrenched ideas.

Listeners were also struck by the manner of Jesus' teaching. He spoke with deep conviction, clear insight and enormous authority. 'He taught as one who had authority, and not as their teachers of the law,' Matthew wrote in his Gospel.

Jesus was aware of his own unique mission and status. He saw himself as greater than some of the great institutions and past leaders of Israel. He also believed that he could perform acts which properly belonged to God — such as forgiving sins and judging the hearts of men and women.

Yet he behaved with humility. He chose ordinary working people as his followers, and he befriended the outcasts of society.

No wonder people thought he was totally unique. They knew he was human, but they still identified him with a whole string of majestic titles: Messiah, Son of God and Lord.

In his teaching, Jesus' constant theme was God and our relationship to him.

Jesus talked about God. He illustrated his teaching from rural life and the world of nature. He rejoiced that we live in a beautiful and exciting world. He knew that we live in a worrying and frightening world, too. Taxes need to be paid; relationships go wrong; possessions are lost or stolen; clothes wear out and food runs out. People get mugged. Accidents happen. Friends die.

Life forces us to ask deep questions — and especially the question: *why?* Why do tragic things happen to innocent people? Do we really find love, purpose and God at the heart of our lives? Or do we live for a mere seventy or so years, in a hostile, meaningless, universe?

To answer such questions, Jesus taught about God as a heavenly Father. Put your trust in him, said Jesus. Keep on praying to him. For God is

▶ *Jesus began his public teaching in Galilee. He chose his first followers from among the local fishermen.*

not distant and uninvolved. He cares. He hears. He loves.

Think of God as a shepherd who guides and protects his flock. Think of God as a Father who loves, and disciplines, his children. Acknowledge God as the supreme lord of everything, including your own individual life. Be generous with your money and with your forgiveness — for God's generosity to you is limitless.

Take those truths deep inside you, and you will never feel the same again — whatever life throws at you. That was the thrust of Jesus' message about God.

Jesus talked about being human. He drew his stories from ordinary life. His teachings illuminated the human heart. But he was not naïve and sentimental. He lived in a harsh world of poverty and fear, violence and greed, bitterness and anger. In his teaching he opposed the values of that world. In his life — and by his death — he confronted the powers of that world.

Jesus loved people. But he was a realist. He knew that there is a lot wrong with human beings. He knew that we need to be rescued from ourselves. And he claimed that he was that rescuer, saying that he came 'not to be served, but to serve, and give his life as a ransom for many'.

5

Another Religious Leader?

Draw up a list of the world's great religious teachers, and Jesus would be included. But should he be? In many ways, Jesus was against religion.

He knew that religion could be dangerous. It could become dry and formal, leading to hypocrisy and bigotry. Jesus wanted to set people free from religion as harsh duty.

He taught that at the heart of true religion we do not find rules and regulations. Instead we find a warm relationship with God as Father, Shepherd and King. Jesus wanted his followers to share God's love by loving the people around them — including the hated Roman overlords and other enemies. It was inevitable that he would clash with the religious leaders of his day.

Jesus had a lot in common with those teachers. Together, they believed in God as Creator and Redeemer. Like him, they thought of God as King and Father — although only Jesus dared to call

Who Was He?

Some of Jesus' claims are very bold. He claimed to forgive sins. He said he would return at the end of time, to judge the world.

At first sight, these are the claims of a conceited fool or a deranged madman. But Jesus' character is marked by deep humility and sanity.

This is a very disturbing mixture for those who want to say that Jesus was 'simply' a good man and a fine teacher.

He wasn't.

Pulling all the evidence together, honest enquirers are forced to decide: either Jesus is to be written off as a blasphemer, or he is to be accepted as the Son of God.

> 'I can see no escape from the dilemma: either Jesus is fraudulent, or his claim is true; either we judge him for being terribly amiss, or we let him judge us.'
> **Michael Ramsey, 100th Archbishop of Canterbury**

God by the intimate family word for Father, *Abba*.
But when it came to the central question, there
was a head-on clash.

'How can I get right with God?' is perhaps
the most important question in the universe. The
religious teachers of Jesus' day came up with the
obvious answer: to get right with God, you must
keep the rules.

That was all right for those who knew what
the rules were. But the regulations had become so
complicated that you needed a degree in theology to
understand them. It was all right for those with
a strong will and an iron self-discipline. And it was
all right for those who didn't look too deeply into
their own hearts.

But what of those who knew themselves to be
moral and spiritual failures?

To these, Jesus came with *bad news* and with
good news.

The bad news was that God's demands are even
harder than they thought. For God is concerned
with our attitudes as well as our actions. In
his famous Sermon on the Mount, Jesus took the
Ten Commandments and made them even tougher.
Murder is wrong, but so is hidden hatred. Adultery
is wrong, but so is secret lust.

The good news is that God loves all of us.
Not just upright religious people, but swindling
business people and prostitutes. Everyone. God's
love embraces us all.

'What a tremendous relief . . . to discover that we don't need to prove ourselves to God. That is what Jesus came to say, and for that he got killed. He came to say, "You don't have to earn God's love. It is not a matter for human achievement. You exist because God loves you already." . . . That is tremendous stuff — that is the Good News.'

Desmond Tutu, Archbishop of Cape Town, South Africa

6

A Perfect Life?

I know some really fine people. They work hard
for others, give generously to important causes and
make others feel good. I know some of their
failings too. Of course, only they know about their
really serious problems: jealousy, pride, pettiness,
self-indulgence. Only they really know themselves.
If you were to ask them whether they were
perfect, they would be amused or appalled.

The author and speaker, C.S. Lewis, was a
highly respected university teacher. But when
he looked deeply into his motives and private
thoughts, he wrote:

> 'For the first time I examined myself with
> a seriously practical purpose. And there I found
> what appalled me: a zoo of lusts, a bedlam
> of ambitions, a nursery of fears, a harem of
> fondled hatreds. My name was legion.'

One person stands out in contrast to all this.

Jesus.

Peter and John were among his first followers. For three years they lived together, worked together, wept together, ate together and shared a common purse. They walked hundreds of miles, got into tight corners, and grew tired together. They knew one another really well. It is remarkable, then, that Peter could apply this Old Testament statement to Jesus: 'he committed no sin, and no deceit was found in his mouth.'

It is just as remarkable that John could write: 'But you know that he appeared so that he might take away our sins. And in him is no sin.'

This does not mean that Jesus was a bland, passionless person. He lived in a tough and violent world. He had strong emotions. He felt joy — and anger, too. But his anger was of the sort which moved Martin Luther King to fight injustice. It was righteous anger, creative anger. It was productive, not destructive.

What about Jesus himself? Would he have laughed — or been appalled — if his friends said he was perfect?

In contrast to every saint who ever lived, the answer is 'no'. Jesus often encouraged other people to confess their sins to God and to seek forgiveness. But we have no record of Jesus ever doing this himself. He seems to have had no personal sense of sin. Was this because he was arrogant or because he was, in fact, perfect?

7

History's Most Important Death?

Near the end of his three years in the public eye, Jesus faced a huge decision. Should he return home, to safety? Or should he go on to Jerusalem, to conflict?

Jesus set out for Jerusalem. That decision led to his death.

Was his a wasted life? In some ways, yes, it was. Jesus had so much to give to the world. And he could have escaped. Had he chosen to travel north to Galilee, not south to Jerusalem, he could have continued his matchless teaching into old age.

But this was not Jesus' intention. Everything he taught and did led to his climactic death. This is especially seen in the dramatic events of his last week of earthly life.

Jesus timed his entry into Jerusalem to coincide with the great Jewish festival of Passover. His reputation ensured a big crowd. But he rode a humble donkey. Here was no worldly king, coming in glittering style to impress and command. Here was the Prince of Peace, riding in humility.

For some days Jesus taught in the precincts of the Temple — a fabulous building erected by King Herod, who had tried to kill Jesus as a baby. Jesus made a direct attack on the attitudes and practices of many of the leaders of his people.

At the Passover festival, the Jewish people gathered in their homes to eat a special supper — a practice which continues today. This was the last meal that Jesus ate with his disciples.

Near the end of the meal, Judas, one of his twelve disciples, left the room and betrayed Jesus to the authorities. They were plotting to arrest Jesus by night — away from the crowds. Although the other disciples swore undying allegiance, Jesus warned them that they too would betray him. He would be killed.

After their meal they sang a hymn and walked out to a garden called Gethsemane on the Mount of Olives. Jesus knew what was coming. He prayed in deep emotion asking that he might be spared the dreadful suffering that the next few hours would bring. But his prayer ended with these famous words, 'Nevertheless, not my will, but yours, be done.'

Shortly after, he was arrested and interrogated through the night by Jewish and Roman courts. Rabble-rousers stirred up the people. Jesus' fate was sealed. No longer did the crowds cry 'Hosanna!' and 'Welcome!' Now they shouted 'Crucify!'

▶ *A mural in the catacombs shows Jesus eating at table with his followers. The first Christians remembered Jesus' Last Supper, and looked forward to meeting finally in heaven.*

Jesus was stripped. Nails were driven through his hands and feet. The cross was then raised, and he was left hanging in the hot sun between two criminals. Soldiers gambled for his single worldly possession: a seamless robe. Later, his side was pierced with a spear to make sure he was dead.

As he was dying, Jesus cried out from the cross, 'Father, forgive them. They don't know what they are doing.'

All Part of a Plan?

Jesus went to Jerusalem knowing it would mean his arrest and crucifixion. The Gospels make it clear that he felt a deep inner conviction. He *must* die in this way.

But why?

He gave the answer at the last meal which he ate with his friends, on the evening of his arrest. Jesus took some wine and said these strange words: 'This is my blood of the covenant, which is poured out for many for the forgiveness of sins.'

Covenant is an important Bible word. It speaks of the love and commitment of God to the world he has made. But the world was no longer as God had intended. God's people had often rejected him and the covenant was in tatters.

Six hundred years before Jesus, the Jewish prophet Jeremiah had promised that, one day, God would make a new covenant with his people. At the Last Supper, Jesus was saying that

The Meaning of the Cross

The Bible devotes a great deal of space to the meaning of Jesus' death.

The Cross reveals the depth of human sin. It was human pride which opposed Jesus; it was human greed which betrayed Jesus; it was human sin which convicted Jesus.

When Jesus died, the land was covered in daytime darkness. It was as though heaven itself was saying: this is the most dreadful day of all.

The Cross reveals the depth of God's love. Rather than using his power to dominate, Jesus chose to submit to the worst that people could do. So the power of God is seen in symbols of weakness — in a manger and on a cross. Here is power kept in check; power handed over; power utterly controlled by love. One of the most famous of Bible quotations begins, 'God so loved the world that he gave his one and only Son . . . '

The cross reveals the difficult demands of Christian discipleship. 'Follow me,' said Jesus. Then he got himself crucified. And

being a Christian always involves a sort of
death. It means:

• holding Jesus' standards in a world which
does not much like those standards,
• trying to care about people when it would
be much easier not to bother,
• trying to change our own wrong attitudes
and habits.

Jesus summed it up like this: 'If anyone
would come after me, he must deny himself
and take up his cross and follow me.'

But paradoxically, Jesus insists that the
cross is about *life* — not only about death.
He goes on to say, 'For whoever wants to
save his life will lose it, but whoever loses his
life for me and for the gospel will save it.'

The cross reveals the way back to God.
As Jesus was dying, he cried out, 'It is
finished.' These words do not mean 'It's all
over'; but 'It is *accomplished*.' He knew
that only his death, the death of the Son
of God, could break down the barriers
of rebellion and indifference which separate
people from their heavenly father and from
one another.

the day had now arrived. He was announcing the new covenant, and he made it clear that:

☐ His own death was the central event in the new covenant.

☐ Forgiveness of sins was the main result of the new covenant.

Many men and women have suffered heroically for others. Yet the Bible says that no one ever suffered as Jesus did. On the cross Jesus suffered physically as the nails were driven home. He suffered emotionally as his friends deserted him. But the Gospels say he suffered spiritually too. This was unique: in dying, he took upon himself the sin of the whole world.

He was broken like bread, and his life was poured out like wine, for the forgiveness of sins.

In the Temple in Jerusalem, a large curtain hung between the Most Holy Place and the rest of the building. It was a symbol of the separation between the holy God and the human race, resulting from our sin.

As Jesus died, that curtain was torn in two from top to bottom. It was a dramatic sign of a new access into the presence of God.

This is a great mystery — but a mystery which has brought light and understanding to countless lives.

'When Jesus came into the world, he loved it so much that he gave his life for it. And what did he do? He made himself the Bread of Life. He became small, fragile, and defenceless for us.'
Mother Teresa

9

Risen Lord?

Only a handful of men have founded great movements. Each of them needed time in which to make his influence felt. For example:

□ Gautama the Buddha (founder of Buddhism). Died in 483BC, age 80.

□ Confucius (the great Chinese teacher). Died in 479BC, age 72.

□ Muhammad (founder of Islam). Died in AD632, age 62.

□ Karl Marx (the intellect behind Communism). Died in AD1883, age 64.

Now compare and *contrast* Jesus Christ. He died in his thirties. He spent only three years in the public eye, in a fairly remote place. Yet the impact of Jesus on history has been even greater than that of the great men listed above.

'There exists such overwhelming
evidence, positive and negative,
factual and circumstantial, that no
intelligent jury in the world could
fail to bring in the verdict that
the resurrection story is true.'
**Lord Darling, former Lord Chief
Justice of England**

How could this village carpenter-turned-preacher make such a colossal impact, given his short life?

Great leaders continue to influence the world, after they are dead, in two ways: through their writings, and through their followers.

Jesus left no writings.

As for his followers, they were shattered when Jesus died. Indeed, they were so frightened that they met behind locked doors. But within days they were totally different: brave, excited, confident and creative. They went preaching in the streets and they told everyone — friend and foe alike — their good news. They had one great theme: 'You crucified Jesus, but God raised him up!' Jesus, they believed, had risen from the dead.

How did they know this? Some of them had visited the tomb of Jesus. It was empty. Others said they had actually seen and touched the risen Christ.

If we examine the disciples' remarkable claims we find three possibilities.

☐ **Were the disciples lying?** They had good reason. After all, they were followers of Jesus, who had died a humiliating death as a criminal. They wanted to rescue his good name. So we can imagine them getting together and cooking up a plot: let's pretend that we have seen him!

This theory comes up against one big problem. Their preaching led them into trouble with the authorities. They were beaten and imprisoned because of it. Some of them were killed.

People will sometimes die for ideas and causes which they believe in passionately. But not for things they have made up. We might suffer for our convictions; we will not willingly suffer for our inventions.

It is significant, too, that the first people who saw Jesus after his death were women. In some countries today, the testimony of a woman carries much less weight than that of a man. This was also true in the Palestine of Jesus' day. If the stories were invented, it is unlikely that such 'lightweight' witnesses would be used.

☐ **Were the disciples mistaken?** It may be that they imagined it all. Perhaps they suffered from hallucinations. People do. But the appearances of Jesus were to many different people, in many different places. And quite often Jesus appeared to groups of witnesses: sometimes ten, sometimes eleven. On one occasion, 500 people saw him.

People can hallucinate in groups — when taking drugs, for example. But each one will see a different hallucination. What people see comes from deep inside the subconscious mind, which differs from person to person much as finger prints do. The disciples all saw the same thing. Or rather they all saw the same person. Jesus.

One further point. The appearances of Jesus soon stopped. But the disciples' conviction that

▶ *The story of Jesus is more than an important event in the past. It is the story of changed lives — now.*

Jesus was alive was reinforced by his *unseen* presence. Their experience of Jesus' spirit has been shared by countless Christians throughout the centuries.

☐ **Were the disciples right?** If the disciples weren't lying, and if they weren't mistaken, we are left with one possibility. It is that possibility which is asserted and explored in the New Testament. Jesus was too good and too great to be held by death. God raised him from the dead.

The evidence for the resurrection of Jesus is remarkably strong. So strong that it has convinced a wide range of people, including lawyers and scientists who are used to sifting data and drawing logical conclusions.

10

Alive Today?

If Jesus really did defeat death, he is alive and active in the modern world. That is the Christian claim. But is it true?

Recently I met three girls who each told a similar story. Each of these girls had been on drugs. To feed their habit they became ruthless and resorted to theft. Then these girls were converted to Christianity.

Their transformation was striking. As they talked about the past it was difficult to recognize the girls they were describing — these girls were caring and honest. People who knew them well vouched for them.

One thing is clear. The revolution in their lives cannot be accounted for in terms of 'turning over a new leaf' or 'pulling themselves together'. They had neither the moral vision nor the spiritual strength to achieve such a radical change. Something happened *to* them.

Each of them describes that 'something' like this. Jesus is alive today. He influenced and changed them — not only by his wonderful teaching and matchless example, but also by his loving presence.

Some of the other evidence for the risen, living Jesus is much less dramatic, but significant just the same. Countless ordinary Christians have an unshakeable sense of being 'accompanied' through life by Jesus.

Often this brings strength and comfort. It sometimes brings a sharp challenge — a challenge to love those we meet, to forgive our enemies, and to serve our troubled and divided world.

Eventually we, too, have to decide. Is this man Jesus uniquely significant? Do we accept him as our liberator and Lord of our lives? Can we write him off as a blasphemous lunatic? Or maybe we can take the easy option: trying to forget his claims about himself and his claims upon us?

> 'Christianity is a statement which, if false, is of *no* importance, and, if true, of infinite importance. The one thing it cannot be is moderately important.' C.S. Lewis

In his teaching, Jesus encourages people to think hard before accepting his invitation to 'Follow me'. But thinking hard is different from sitting on the fence. Eventually we have to make up our minds.

We have put Jesus on trial. But if he really is the Son of God, as we come to our verdict, it is *we* who are being tried by *him*.